10654135

would like to thank all those who have helped us in the
paration of this book, particularly:
ert Bearman, Senior Archivist, Shakespeare Birthplace
t, and all the restaurateurs and chefs listed on pages 61
63 who have so kindly provided us with recipes.

To my parents,
who epitomize all that is best
in England,
with love

RD'S MEMORIAL, TRINITY CHURCH is illustrated on
ious page. His epitaph reads:
frend for Jesus sake forbeare,
the dust encloased heare;
e ye man yt spares thes stones,
st be he yt moves my bones."

ished 1981 by
dwards Limited,
Mow Passage,
/4.

ISBN 0 904330 68 0
Second Impression, April 1982
Printed in England by
T.J. Press (Padstow) Ltd.

We
pre
Rob
Tru

The
Creative
Hostess

STRATFO[
UPON
AVON
COOKBOO[

THE BA
the pre
"Good
To digg
Bleste [
And cu[

© Copyri

First pub
Marion E
10 Barley
London V

The
Creative Hostess
STRATFORD
UPON
AVON
COOKBOOK

WITH
DRAWINGS OF THE TOWN
BY
GERALDINE
MARCHAND

Introduction

"'Tis an ill cook that cannot lick his own fingers."
ROMEO AND JULIET IV.ii.6.

. . . which is just what we aim to tempt you to do with this lovely collection of recipes.

Stratford-upon-Avon, the birthplace and home of William Shakespeare, attracts visitors from all over the world. Some have stayed to make their homes here — among them a talented collection of chefs, who find it a challenge to tempt the palate of the tired sightseer and send him home with tales not only of sights seen but also of memorable meals enjoyed in the very heart of England.

Within these pages are gathered together traditional fare and restaurant favourites. Just follow the step-by-step instructions from the chefs of Stratford, and you can recreate with ease the dishes of the masters!

But this little book has something more to offer. Dip into it and you will find that the recipes are interspersed with evocative drawings of Stratford's Tudor buildings and interesting things we think you might like to know about this fascinating town.

Join us on a tour of Stratford and share with us some of its best culinary secrets.

Contents

A note on measures & conversions
Ingredients are given in metric, Imperial and American measures. **Use measures from one column only.** Teaspoon and tablespoon measures in the metric column correspond to 5 ml and 15 ml respectively.

Shakespeare's Stratford

It is perhaps appropriate that the English language's greatest writer should have come from the "Heart of England". Queen Elizabeth I had been on the throne for six years when William Shakespeare came into the world in Henley Street, Stratford-upon-Avon. Now standing by itself, the house where the Shakespeares lived would have been one of a row of buildings. John Shakespeare, William's father, was a glover and wool merchant; he used part of the house for his business and the rest to live in.

Like the birthplace, many of Stratford's buildings are much as Shakespeare would have seen them (although the timbered fronts owe much to careful restoration by the removal of plaster and stone wall coverings which were fashionable in the 18th century). The timber-framed houses were naturally very susceptible to fire and many were destroyed this way, despite the requirement that each household should have a leather bucket full of water at the ready!

From his home in Henley Street, the young Shakespeare would have walked to school in Church Street, passing on the way the then private houses now known as Harvard House, the Garrick Inn and Falcon Hotel.

As William grew up, his interest turned to the nearby village of Shottery, where he was a regular visitor at the Hathaway household. From Henley Street he would walk across the fields to court Anne, eight years his senior, whom he married when he was eighteen. You can follow the same route today.

Although Anne and William came from similar artisan backgrounds (Anne's father being a yeoman farmer) the prosperity of the Shakespeare family had begun to decline when William was about eleven, to the extent that his father was "left untaxed" in 1578. It is probable that the family's lack of money (not to mention the three children he had to support by the time he was twenty-one) led William to seek his fortune—like Dick Whittington—in London. His success in the big city made him a wealthy man, and he invested his money wisely in property. For a home, he purchased one of the largest houses in Stratford, New Place. Clearly, the residence was a very grand one—when Queen Henrietta Maria was on her way to meet King Charles I in 1643 she stayed at the house, then occupied by Shakespeare's daughter, Susanna. The foundations are all that now remain.

Some aspects of life in Tudor Stratford have changed very little, considering that 400 years have passed. For instance, the Shakespeares would have crossed the Avon over the same stone bridge that you do today, while John Shakespeare would have bought the leather skins for his trade at Rothermarket—on the same site that a weekly market currently occupies. The annual "Mop" fair is still held in the town centre on October 12th. This was the day when servants would offer their services for hire. The name "Mop" refers to the mop, or other indication of a trade, that potential employees would display. A couple of weeks later a "runaway mop" took place, to give servants the opportunity to change their employer. By all accounts, this was fortunately a much smaller event than the first fair! Nowadays, the "Mop" is just as lively an occasion, with the roasting of a pig, country dancing and singing, and stalls—probably not such a very different scene from the fairs held in Shakespeare's day.

THE GOWER MEMORIAL

Unveiled in 1888 to cheers from the watching crowd, the monument in Bancroft Gardens took sculptor Lord Ronald Gower twelve years to complete.

Around the monument are life-size bronzes of some of Shakespeare's characters: Prince Hal symbolising history, Falstaff representing comedy, Lady Macbeth, tragedy, and Hamlet, philosophy.

There are thirteen other Stratfords in the world, eight of them in the USA. The most famous is in Ontario, Canada, notable for having a distinguished Shakespeare season of its own. Other Stratfords are to be found in London, the North Island of New Zealand, Quebec and in the State of Victoria, Australia.

SHAKESPEARE'S BIRTHPLACE

William's father, John Shakespeare, first used the right-hand part of the house in Henley Street as an office and subsequently bought the adjoining house for the family to live in.

Today, signatures inscribed on the windows of the first-floor room in which Shakespeare was born bear witness to the famous visitors to the house. Among them are Walter Scott, Thomas Carlyle, Henry Irving and Ellen Terry.

STILTON AND PORT PATE

Serves 4

An old English recipe from the Swan's Nest Hotel.

Metric		lb/oz	U.S.A.
125 g	*Stilton cheese*	5 oz	5 oz
1 tbsp	*Butter*	1 tbsp	1 tbsp
1 tbsp	*Flour*	1 tbsp	1 tbsp
8	*Black olives, finely chopped*	8	8
100 ml	*Port*	1 oz	¼ cup
	Garlic to taste		
50 g	*Mayonnaise*	2 oz	¼ cup
100 ml	*Double cream*	⅛ pt	¼ cup
50 g	*Clarified butter**	2 oz	¼ cup

1. Crumble the cheese into a bowl.
2. Melt the butter and add the flour. Cook for 2 – 3 minutes, stirring all the time.
3. Add the butter to the Stilton.
4. Add the olives to the Stilton with the port, garlic and freshly ground pepper. Season to taste and mix well.
5. Stir in the mayonnaise and cream.
6. Beat with a whisk until creamy, then pour into individual moulds and cover with melted clarified butter.
7. Place in the refrigerator to set.
8. Serve with toast or savoury biscuits either at the table or with pre-dinner drinks.

To clarify butter, melt over a gentle heat. Remove and set aside until the milky solids settle. Skim the clarified butter from the top and transfer to a covered bowl. Refrigerate until needed.

SANCTUARY KNOCKER *(above)* As you enter Holy Trinity Church by the north porch, on an inner door you will see this curious iron ring, thought to be more than 600 years old. Criminals, especially fast runners, were very grateful for the sanctuary knocker which protected them from arrest as long as they were holding on to it!

MERRY WIVES CRAB PUFFS   *Makes 24*

Make merry with your guests! These tasty savouries can be made early in the day and frozen until shortly before your guests arrive in the evening.

Metric		lb/oz	U.S.A.
3 tbsp	Mayonnaise	3 tbsp	4 tbsp
80 g	Philadelphia cream cheese	3 oz	½ cup
2 drops	Tabasco sauce	2 drops	2 drops
1 tbsp	Parmesan cheese	1 tbsp	1 tbsp
100 g	Crabmeat	4 oz	½ cup
3	Spring onions, finely chopped	3	3
1	Egg white	1	1
6	Bread slices	6	6
	For the topping:		
2 tbsp	Parmesan cheese	2 tbsp	2 tbsp
2 tsp	Paprika	2 tsp	2 tsp

1. Mix together the mayonnaise, cream cheese, Tabasco sauce and Parmesan cheese.
2. Chop the crabmeat and stir into the mixture with the onions.
3. Beat the egg white stiffly and fold into the mixture.
4. Cut the bread slices into four, removing crusts. Toast on one side and spread each round with crab paste on the other.
5. Coat the crab mixture with the cheese and paprika topping and place on a baking tray. Put in the freezer for 2-3 hours, removing half an hour before needed.
6. Before serving, place the tray under the grill until the tops are golden brown.

POTTED SALMON   *Serves 8*

Metric		lb/oz	U.S.A.
500 g	Cooked salmon	1 lb	1 lb
175 g	Clarified butter (see p.10)	6 oz	1 cup
1 tsp	Cayenne pepper	1 tsp	1 tsp
1 tsp	Ground mace	1 tsp	1 tsp

1. Remove the skin and bones from the fish and break up into small pieces.
2. Gradually add half the clarified butter, the cayenne pepper and the ground mace. Season to taste.
3. Press the mixture into small pots or ramekins.
4. Top the potted salmon with the remaining clarified butter and put in the refrigerator to set.
5. Serve with toast or savoury biscuits either at the table or with pre-dinner drinks.

HOLY TRINITY CHURCH

This view shows the silver birch planted in memory of the actress Vivien Leigh. Her plaque is inscribed with the Poet's words from Antony and Cleopatra—*"A lass unparallel'd"*

In Holy Trinity Church, a copy of the parish register records Shakespeare's baptism in April 1564 and burial in April 1616.

BACON AND OYSTER BITES

This is an easy savoury which can be made with fresh or smoked (canned) oysters. Serve with pre-dinner drinks or as an after dinner savoury.

1. You will need two oysters for each rasher of bacon. Use a fairly lean cut of bacon. Trim the rind off the bacon and "stretch" each rasher with the back of a knife.
2. Cut each rasher in half. Drain the oysters, sprinkle with paprika (if available) and wrap a piece of bacon around each one. Secure with a wooden cocktail stick.
3. Grill the savouries two minutes on each side.

MISERICORDS

Look underneath the hinged seats of the choir stalls at Holy Trinity Church and you will find some amusing carvings, like this one of St George and the dragon. Other misericords show a mermaid holding a mirror while combing her hair and a housewife hitting her husband over the head with a saucepan!

Tradition has it that Ben Jonson visited Shakespeare shortly before his death aged fifty-two. He died on his birthday, April 23rd (St George's Day) in 1616.

BAKED AVOCADO FRUITS DE MER   *Serves 2*

A succulent hot starter from the Shakespeare Hotel.

Metric		*lb/oz*	*U.S.A.*
1	*Ripe avocado*	1	1
50 g	*Butter*	2 oz	⅛ cup
30 g	*Peeled prawns*	1 oz	¼ cup
2 tbsp	*White wine*	2 tbsp	3 tbsp
80 g	*Double cream*	3 oz	¼ cup
20 g	*Smoked salmon or shellfish, chopped*	½ oz	2 tbsp
2 tbsp	*Cream sherry*	2 tbsp	3 tbsp
	To garnish:		
	Lettuce, cucumber and lemon wedges		

1. Cut the avocado in half, remove the flesh with a teaspoon and cut into 2 cm (½") cubes. Keep the avocado skins.
2. Melt half the butter in a small pan and quickly sauté the prawns.
3. Add the white wine and boil to reduce, then add the cream allowing that to reduce.
4. Add the avocado and salmon to the cream. Add the sherry and bring to the boil quickly while adding the remaining butter in small knobs. (This helps to thicken the mixture and gives the sauce a shine.)
5. Place the mixture back into the avocado skins and serve on a bed of lettuce with cucumber and a wedge of lemon.

EVESHAM ASPARAGUS   *Serves 4*

A summer favourite at the Swan's Nest Hotel.

Metric		*lb/oz*	*U.S.A.*
500 g	*Asparagus*	1 lb	1 lb
½	*Lemon, juice of*	½	½

1. Put on a tall saucepan of water to boil.
2. Scrape the bark from the bottom of the asparagus.
3. Tie the asparagus into a bundle to fit the pot. Add the lemon juice and a pinch of salt to the boiling water.
4. Stand the asparagus stems (not tips) in the water as upright as possible, covering the pan with a lid. Cook for 5 – 15 minutes, depending upon the stalks' thickness.
5. When cooked, remove from the water, take off the string and arrange portions on plates.
6. Serve with lemon butter sauce.

Lemon butter sauce

Metric		lb/oz	U.S.A.
80 g	Unsalted or clarified butter (see p.10)	3 oz	⅓ cup
1 tbsp	Chopped parsley	1 tbsp	1 tbsp
1	Lemon, juice of	1	1
	Freshly ground black pepper		

1. Put the butter in a saucepan and melt slowly.
2. Stir in the parsley, lemon juice and pepper.

"This is fairy gold."   THE WINTER'S TALE III. iii. 127.

DEEP-FRIED MUSHROOM CUPS
CHAMPIGNONS LANGUEDOCIENNE   *Serves 2*

A delicious combination of mushroom and pâté from the Buccaneer Restaurant.

Metric		lb/oz	U.S.A.
250 g	Mushrooms, closed cup	8 oz	2 cups
50 g	Pâté	2 oz	¼ cup
1	Egg, beaten	1	1
50 g	Breadcrumbs	2 oz	½ cup
	Oil for frying		

1. Wash the mushrooms. Remove the stalks but do not peel.
2. Blanch in boiling salted water for 2–3 minutes. Remove and allow to cool.
3. Stuff the mushrooms with the pâté.
4 Brush all over with beaten egg and coat with breadcrumbs. Shake gently to remove any loose breadcrumbs.
5. Deep fry in oil until golden brown. Drain on kitchen paper. Place on a warm dish and serve with piquant sauce.*

*A creamy horseradish dressing can be substituted if time is short. Editor.

Piquant sauce   *Makes 300ml (½ pt, 1 cup)*

Metric		lb/oz	U.S.A.
50 g	Shallots, chopped	2 oz	½ cup
80 ml	Vinegar	⅛ pt	¼ cup
300 ml	Demi-glace sauce (p.16)	½ pt	1 cup
30 g	Gherkins, chopped	1 oz	¼ cup
20 g	Caper, chopped	½ oz	2 tbsp
½ tbsp	Chervil, chopped	½ tbsp	½ tbsp
½ tbsp	Tarragon, chopped	½ tbsp	½ tbsp
½ tbsp	Parsley, chopped	½ tbsp	½ tbsp

1. Place the shallots and vinegar in a saucepan and boil until the liquid reduces by half.
2. Add the demi-glace and simmer gently for 15–20 minutes.
3. Add the rest of the ingredients. Stir to heat through. Season to taste.

16

Demi-glace sauce

To make a demi-glace sauce, put equal quantities of
Espagnole sauce (below) and strong beef stock into a heavy
pan (with a few mushrooms if available).
Simmer until the sauce is reduced by at least half. Remove,
strain and re-heat. Remove from the heat and stir in a small
glassful of dry sherry.

Espagnole sauce

Metric		lb/oz	U.S.A.
25 g	Ham or bacon (raw), chopped	1 tbsp	1 tbsp
25 g	Butter	1 oz	1 tbsp
1	Carrot, peeled and chopped	1	1
1	Onion	1	1
3 tbsp	Mushroom stalks, chopped	3 tbsp	4 tbsp
2 tbsp	Celery, chopped (optional)	2 tbsp	3 tbsp
1	Beef stock cube	1	1
1 tsp	Thyme	1 tsp	1 tsp
1	Bay leaf	1	1
40 g	Flour	1 ½ oz	¼ cup
2 tbsp	Tomato paste	2 tbsp	3 tbsp
250 g	Tomatoes, peeled and chopped	½ lb	2 cups

1. Cook the bacon in the butter for a few minutes.
2. Add the vegetables and sauté gently for 5 – 8 minutes.
3. Make a stock with the cube and 300ml (½ pt) boiling
   water, and set aside.
4. Stir the flour into the vegetable mixture. Continue stirring
   until the flour browns well, then add the stock very
   gradually, stirring continuously.
5. When the sauce has thickened, stir in the tomato paste,
   tomatoes, thyme and bay leaf. Season lightly.
6. Simmer for 30 minutes, stirring occasionally and skimming
   off excess fat. Taste and correct the seasoning.
7. Strain the sauce into a basin and cover the surface with
   damp greaseproof paper or clingwrap to prevent a skin
   forming.

CELERY, APPLE AND TOMATO SOUP   *Serves 4*

A delicious soup from the Swan's Nest Hotel.

Metric		lb/oz	U.S.A.
1	Can of celery, large	1	1
1	Stick of fresh celery	1	1
2	Red apples	2	2
4	Tomatoes	4	4
80 g	Butter	3 oz	⅓ cup
2	Onions	2	2
30 g	Flour	1 oz	¼ cup
150 ml	Single cream	¼ pt	½ cup

1. Place the canned celery and liquid from can in a liquidiser and purée.
2. Chop the fresh celery and boil in a little salted water until tender. Remove from heat, but do not drain.
3. Peel, core and dice the apples.
4. Skin the tomatoes (drop in boiling water for a few seconds or rotate on the end of a fork over a gas flame). Remove the seeds and chop up the flesh.
5. Melt the butter gently in a saucepan* and sauté the onion until soft, then add flour and cook for 3 – 4 minutes until lightly coloured. Stir frequently.
6. Add the celery purée, bring to the boil and simmer for 5 minutes.
7. Add the apple and tomato, and season to taste.
8. Stir in the cooked celery and liquid.
9. Lastly, add the cream. Heat again but do not boil, and serve immediately.

If you reduce the quantity of butter slightly and add a little oil, the chances of the butter burning are greatly reduced. Editor.

SOLOMUGUNDY   *Serves 8-10*

"My salad days/When I was green in judgment."
ANTONY AND CLEOPATRA: I.v. 673.

A popular Elizabethan salad from the Falcon Hotel.

Metric		lb/oz	U.S.A.
500 g	Chicken, cooked	1 lb	1 lb
1.5 kg	Apples, sliced	3 lb	3 lb
600 ml	Mayonnaise	1 pt	2 cups
1	Stick of celery, diced	1	1
250 g	Walnuts, shelled and chopped	8 oz	1 ½ cups
1	Onion, diced	1	1
1	Lettuce	1	1
½	Cucumber, sliced	½	½
500 g	Tomatoes	1 lb	1 lb
250 g	Beetroot, diced	8 oz	8 oz

1. Break the chicken into small pieces and add with the apples to the mayonnaise. Mix well.
2. Stir in the celery, walnuts and onions and season to taste.
3. Spread the lettuce on a serving plate, and garnish round the edge with cucumber and tomatoes.
4. Spoon the mayonnaise mixture into the centre and place the beetroot on top.

THE SEVEN AGES OF MAN are depicted on the sundial base by the Knott Garden in New Place.

Main Dishes

CHICORY AND HAM MORNAY   *Serves 2*

A hot bistro dish from the Boathouse Wine Bar.

Metric		lb/oz	U.S.A.
	4 small heads of chicory		
	4 slices of ham		
	For the cheese sauce:		
20 g	Butter	¾ oz	2 tbsp
20 g	Flour	¾ oz	2 tbsp
300 ml	Creamy milk	½ pint	1 cup
75 g	Hard cheese, grated	3 oz	¾ cup
1	Cayenne pepper, pinch of	1	1
1	Dried mustard, pinch of	1	1
	Freshly ground pepper		
60 g	Cheddar cheese, grated	2 oz	½ cup

1. Cook the chicory in lightly salted boiling water until tender.
2. To make the cheese sauce, melt the butter in a saucepan and stir in the flour. Cook gently for one minute.
3. Add the milk a little at a time, stirring continuously.
4. Add the hard cheese, cayenne pepper, mustard and freshly ground pepper. Stir well and cook for two minutes to a good pouring consistency. Season to taste.
5. Drain the chicory well and wrap each piece in a slice of ham. Pack tightly in a serving dish, pour over the sauce and sprinkle the grated cheese on top.
6. Bake in a moderate oven, 180°C, 350°F, Gas Mark 4, for 10 minutes to reheat and place under a hot grill for a few minutes to brown the top.
7. Serve with toast triangles or crusty bread.

SCHOOL CLOCK *(above)* Perhaps it was the memory of long hours at his school desk which led Shakespeare to write in JULIUS CAESAR, *"The clock hath stricken three"* — now probably literature's most famous anachronism, as clocks had yet to be invented!

PRAWN AND CHIVE QUICHE   *Serves 4*

A light and pretty supper dish from the Hathaway Tea Rooms.

Metric		lb/oz	U.S.A.
200 g	Shortcrust pastry	8 oz	8 oz
175 g	Cheese, grated	6 oz	6 oz
100 g	Prawns	4 oz	4 oz
2 tbsp	Chives, chopped	2 tbsp	3 tbsp
6	Eggs	6	6
300 ml	Milk	½ pt	1 cup
150 ml	Cream	¼ pt	½ cup
8	Tomato slices	8	8
1 tbsp	Chives, chopped	1 tbsp	tbsp

1. Line a 25cm (10") greased flan dish with pastry and cover with grated cheese, prawns and chives.
2. Beat the eggs, milk and cream together, season to taste, and pour over the flan.
3. Decorate with slices of tomato and chopped chives.
4. Bake at 190°C, 375°F, Gas Mark 5 for 35 – 40 minutes.

QUICHE CREOLE   *Serves 6*

A tasty creation from the chef of the Grosvenor House Hotel.

Metric		lb/oz	U.S.A.
200 g	Flour	8 oz	2 cups
100 g	Butter	4 oz	½ cup
1 tbsp	Lemon juice	1 tbsp	1 tbsp
4	Eggs	4	4
600 ml	Milk	1 pt	2 ½ cups
200 g	Chicken, cooked and sliced	8 oz	8 oz
1	Tomato, chopped	1	1
50 g	Ham, cut into strips	2 oz	2 oz
4	Spring onions, finely chopped	4	4
1	Green pepper, chopped	1	1
50 g	Mushrooms	2 oz	¾ cup
1	Clove of garlic, crushed	1	1

1. Put flour into a bowl with a pinch of salt. Rub in the fat until it resembles breadcrumbs. Add lemon juice to make a soft dough and leave in a cool place for half an hour.
2. Roll out the pastry and line a 20 cm (8") greased flan tin.
3. Whisk the eggs and milk until light and fluffy. Season to taste.
4. Add the chicken, tomato, ham, onions, green peppers, mushrooms and garlic.
5. Pour the mixture into the pastry case and bake in a pre-heated oven for 35 minutes at 180°C, 350 °F, Gas Mark 4.

SANGANAKI A LA PEREA   *Serves 3*

A favourite at both the Shakespeare Hotel and Alveston Manor.

Metric		lb/oz	U.S.A.
500 g	*Scampi*	1 lb	1 lb
100 g	*Mushrooms*	4 oz	15
3	*Artichoke bottoms (cooked)*	3	3
100 g	*Fetta or goats' milk cheese*	4 oz	4 oz
2 tbsp	*Oil for frying*	2 tbsp	3 tbsp
150 ml	*Cream sherry*	¼ pt	½ cup
200 ml	*Double cream*	⅓ pt	¾ cup

1. Wash, peel and quarter the mushrooms and artichoke bottoms. Cut cheese into 2 cm (½") cubes.
2. Quickly sauté the scampi in the oil for 2 – 3 minutes and remove from the pan.
3. In the same pan sauté the mushrooms and when almost cooked add the artichoke bottoms.
4. Add the sherry, reduce a little and add the cream, and bring to the boil, stirring all the time to thicken.
5. Replace the scampi for a minute and, just before serving, add the diced cheese. Serve on a bed of rice.

SOLE OLD ENGLAND   *Serves 2*

An aromatic fish creation from the Swan's Nest Hotel.

Metric		lb/oz	U.S.A.
	4 sole fillets		
100 g	*Smoked mackerel flesh*	4 oz	4 oz
2	*Shallots, finely chopped*	2	2
1 tsp	*Parsley, chopped*	1 tsp	1 tsp
1 tsp	*Thyme, chopped*	1 tsp	1 tsp
1	*Tarragon, pinch of*	1	1
350 g	*Puff pastry*	12 oz	12 oz
1	*Egg yolk*	1	1
	For the parsley sauce:		
300 ml	*Milk*	½ pt	1 cup
1 tbsp	*Cornflour*	1 tbsp	1 tbsp
1 tbsp	*Parsley, chopped*	1 tbsp	1 tbsp

"I know a bank whereon the wild thyme blows."

A MIDSUMMER NIGHT'S
DREAM II.i.249.

WOMEN'S LIB IN
HOLY TRINITY! (see page 13)

1. Remove skin from sole fillets.
2. Mince mackerel, mix with shallots, parsley, thyme, tarragon and season with salt and pepper.
3. Spread the filling on two sole fillets and cover with remaining two.
4. Roll the pastry into a rectangular shape and cut in half.
5. Place a fillet on top of each portion, damp, fold and pinch the edges.
6. Brush pastry all over with egg yolk. Bake in a fairly hot oven, 210°C, 425°F, Gas Mark 7, for 15 – 20 minutes.
7. To make the parsley sauce, boil the milk.
8. Mix the cornflour with a little cold milk and stir into the boiling milk. Continue stirring until the sauce thickens.
9. Add the parsley and stir well. Serve sauce separately.

CHEF VALLADE'S SOLE SPECIALITY
FRICASSEE DE SOLE AUX MOULES A LA CREME
DE SAFFRAN   *Serves 4*

A delicious fish dish from the Welcombe Hotel. Lemon sole can be substituted if Dover sole is not available.

Metric		*lb/oz*	*U.S.A.*
	4 fillets of Dover sole		
600 ml	*Mussels*	1 pt	1 pt
2	*Shallots, finely chopped*	2	2
300 ml	*Dry white wine*	½ pt	1 cup
100 g	*Leeks*	4 oz	1 cup
30 g	*Butter*	1 oz	2 tbsp
150 ml	*Double cream*	¼ pt	½ cup
½ tsp	*Saffron*	½ tsp	½ tsp
2 tbsp	*Parsley, chopped*	2 tbsp	2 tbsp

1. Clean the mussels and discard any broken ones. Place in a saucepan with the shallots and wine. Cook for 5 – 10 minutes until all the mussels have opened. Discard any that do not open.
2. When the mussels have cooled a little, remove them from the shells and keep warm. Reserve the stock.
3. Clean and trim the leeks, and cut into very thin strips, 5 – 8 cm (2 – 3 in) long. Blanch in boiling salted water for a few minutes. Do not overcook. Remove and keep warm.
4. Cut the sole into strips. Melt the butter gently in a frying pan and sauté the sole. Add the stock and bring to the boil. Remove the sole and add to the mussels.
5. Boil the stock until it has reduced by half. Remove from the heat and stir in the double cream. Reduce until the sauce has thickened.
6. Add the saffron and season to taste.
7. Put the sole and mussels into a serving dish. Cover them with the sauce and sprinkle with the leeks and parsley.

PAUPIETTES DU VEAU AUX SAUMON FUME — *Serves 8*

Created to include all the things the Buccaneers chef's wife likes best, this dish is a small masterpiece.

Metric		lb/oz	U.S.A.
	8 escalopes of veal		
	8 smoked salmon slices		
	8 asparagus spears, cooked		
50 g	Butter	2 oz	¼ cup
100 g	Mushrooms, sliced	4 oz	1 cup
1	White wine, small glass	1	1
1	Brandy, measure	1	1
150 ml	Single cream	¼ pt	½ cup
2 tbsp	Parsley, chopped	2 tbsp	3 tbsp

1. Beat out the escalopes of veal with a wooden mallet or with the end of a rolling pin.
2. Place a slice of salmon on top of each escalope.
3. Lay one asparagus spear on the top of each piece of salmon and roll up. Secure with a wooden cocktail stick.
4. Melt the butter in a frying pan and gently sauté the veal rolls for about 10 minutes until they are golden brown. Remove and place on a warm serving dish in a low oven.
5. To make the sauce, add mushrooms to pan and sauté gently. Add the wine and boil for a few minutes to reduce.
6. If the sauce is too thin, thicken slightly with 1 tbsp cornflour. Add the brandy, remove from the heat and add the cream. Season to taste.
7. Remove the sticks from the paupiettes and arrange on a bed of rice. Cover with sauce and garnish with parsley.

ESCALOPES PIEMONTESE — *Serves 4*

This tasty dish, from the chef of Da Giovanni Restaurant, takes its name from a mountainous region in northern Italy.

Metric		lb/oz	U.S.A.
	8 small veal escalopes		
1	Egg, beaten	1	1
4 tbsp	Breadcrumbs	4 tbsp	5 tbsp
50 g	Butter	2 oz	¼ cup
250 g	Asparagus	½ lb	½ lb
250 g	Mushrooms, chopped	½ lb	½ lb
2 tbsp	Tomato purée	2 tbsp	3 tbsp
1	Garlic clove, crushed	1	1
1 tsp	Basil	1 tsp	1 tsp
4 tbsp	Parmesan cheese	4 tbsp	5 tbsp
2 tbsp	Parsley, chopped	2 tbsp	2 tbsp

1. Flatten the meat using a wooden mallet or rolling pin.
2. Brush all over with beaten egg and coat with breadcrumbs. Fry in half the butter. Remove and keep warm.

3. Cook the asparagus as described on page 14. Drain and chop into small pieces.
4. Melt the remaining butter in the pan and sauté the mushrooms. Remove from the heat and add the chopped asparagus, tomato purée, garlic and basil.
5. Place four of the escalopes in an oven-proof serving dish, spoon a little of the sauce over each one, and sprinkle with half the Parmesan.
6. Place the remaining escalopes on top, pour over the rest of the sauce and sprinkle each one with Parmesan.
7. Bake in a moderate oven, 180°C, 350°F, Gas Mark 4, for 15 – 20 minutes. Sprinkle with parsley before serving.

MEDAILLONS DE PORC SELINA   *Serves 4*

The joke's in the yolk in this fun recipe which the chef of the Rose and Crown Restaurant prepares for special menus.

Metric		lb/oz	U.S.A.
	4 pork fillets		
2 tbsp	Seasoned flour	2 tbsp	3 tbsp
1	Egg, beaten	1	1
2 tbsp	Breadcrumbs	2 tbsp	3 tbsp
50 g	Butter	2 oz	¼ cup
	For the sauce:		
2	Egg yolks	2	2
2 tsp	Lemon juice	2 tsp	2 tsp
1	Bay leaf	1	1
1 tbsp	Vinegar	1 tbsp	1 tbsp
1 tsp	English mustard	1 tsp	1 tsp
	Freshly ground pepper		
100 g	Butter	4 oz	½ cup
4	Apricot halves	4	4

1. Cut pork fillets into rounds, and beat with a wooden mallet or the end of a rolling pin until thin. Dust in seasoned flour, brush with beaten egg and cover with breadcrumbs.
2. Melt the butter gently in a frying pan and fry the pork slices until cooked. Place on a heated dish and keep warm.
3. Place the egg yolks with the lemon juice, bay leaf, vinegar, mustard and pepper in a bowl over a saucepan of hot water. Whisk all the time until the whisk leaves a trail.
4. Cut the butter into small pieces and add a piece at a time to the bowl. Continue whisking all the time. When all the butter is used up, the sauce will be thick. Whisk in 1 tbsp of cold water. This will give a shine to the sauce.
5. Place the medallions around the edge of a large serving plate, overlapping each one. Pour the sauce into the centre.
6. Place the apricot halves into the sauce to give the impression of fried eggs.
7. Place the dish under the grill to glaze lightly.

THE GRAMMAR SCHOOL,
GUILDHALL & ALMSHOUSES

These buildings look very much as they would have done when the young Shakespeare attended the school. They were built in the 15th century by the Guild of The Holy Cross, founded two hundred years before. The Almshouses continue to be occupied by elderly local people.

Discipline was strict at the school and boys were encouraged to learn with the help of regular beatings. You can see the desk at which Shakespeare learned "little Latin and small Greek" at his birthplace.

"*And then the whining school-boy, with his satchel / And shining morning face, creeping like snail Unwillingly to school.*"
AS YOU LIKE IT II.vii.145.

TERRINE DE POULET LAURETTA OKAGBUE   *Serves 8*

A dish created by Marlowe's for the great-niece of Sir Henry Lightfoot-Boston, later Governor General of Sierre Leone. This dish may be ordered specially.

Metric		lb/oz	U.S.A.
	2 fresh chickens, each		
1.5 kg	weighing	3½ lb	3½ lb
1	Spanish onion, small, quartered	1	1
1	Garlic clove, (or more according to taste)	1	1
2	Sprigs fresh basil, chopped	2	2
2	Sprigs fresh tarragon, chopped	2	2
1	Dried mixed herbs, pinch of	1	1
30 g	Butter	1 oz	2 tbsp
	For the sauce:		
30 g	Dried juniper berries	1 oz	¼ cup
2	Measures of gin	2	2
4	Avocados, ripe	4	4
3	Sprigs parsley, chopped	3	3
1	Bunch of watercress, chopped	1	1

1. Place the juniper berries in the gin.
2. Remove all the bones and skin from both chickens and keep white (breast) and dark flesh separate.
3. Mince the dark chicken flesh coarsely, together with the onion and garlic, then blend all the herbs into the mixture. Season to taste.
4. Slice the white flesh into 5 mm (¼") thick broad slices.
5. Generously brush a loaf tin with butter and place alternate layers of white and dark flesh. Cover with foil.
6. Place loaf tin into larger baking tray half filled with cold water and put in a moderate oven, 170°C, 325°F, Gas Mark 3 for 1¼ hours. Cool before turning out.
7. Refrigerate for not less than three hours then serve sliced, showing layered effect.
8. To make the sauce, peel and de-stone the avocados. Strain the juniper berries, reserving the gin.
9. Pass the avocados and juniper berries through a medium-fine sieve.
10. Extract juice of parsley and watercress separately by squeezing through a cloth. Add these juices to the avocado purée then add enough of the gin to make a sauce that coats the back of a spoon. Season to taste.
11. To serve, use a 20 cm (8") plate with a rim (plain white if possible). Pour on sufficient sauce to cover the bottom of the plate, then place a slice of terrine in the middle of the sauce. Garnish with a tomato rose. (To make a tomato rose, cut a strip of skin from around a tomato, and curl neatly into a "rose".)

SUPREME OF CHICKEN WITH
FRESH ASPARAGUS   *Serves 4*

A popular light and luscious dish from the Stratford Hilton.

Metric		lb/oz	U.S.A.
750 g	Asparagus	1 ½ lb	1 ½ lb
4	Chicken breasts	4	4
50 g	Butter	2 oz	¼ cup
	Asparagus stock		
3 tbsp	White wine	3 tbsp	4 tbsp
150 ml	Double cream	¼ pt	½ cup
4	Fresh tarragon, sprigs	4	4

1. Cook the asparagus as described on page 14. Drain and reserve the liquid. Put the asparagus on a plate and keep warm. Reduce the stock to 300 ml (½ pt, 1 cup).
2. Sauté the chicken breasts in the butter. Add the asparagus stock and white wine, and re-heat.
3. Add the cream and half the tarragon, cover the pan and gently simmer.
4. When the meat is cooked, remove and set aside. Reduce the sauce a little more if necessary. Season and strain.
5. Cut each breast into five slices and place on asparagus. Coat with sauce and garnish with fresh tarragon.

AIGUILLETTES OF CHICKEN INDIENNE   *Serves 2*

A spicy delight from the Shakespeare Hotel.

Metric		lb/oz	U.S.A.
	2 Chicken breasts (supremes)		
1 tsp	Mild curry powder	1 tsp	1 tsp
5 – 10 ml	Jeera (ground cumin) powder	1-2 tsp	1-2 tsp
20 g	Onion, finely diced	½ oz	2 tbsp
15 ml	Oil for cooking	1 tbsp	1 tbsp
1	Clove of garlic, crushed	1	1
100 ml	White wine	⅛ pt	¼ cup
150 ml	Double cream	¼ pt	½ cup
	To serve:		
100 g	Rice	4 oz	½ cup
30 g	Sultanas	1 oz	¼ cup
30 g	Roasted flaked almonds	1 oz	¼ cup

1. Cut each supreme into 4 or 5 thin strips.
2. Place on a plate and rub in the curry and cumin powder. Season with salt and pepper.
3. Fry the onions in the oil until transparent but not brown — add the garlic and pieces of chicken and stir in the pan for a few minutes. Add the white wine, allowing it to reduce a little before adding the cream.
4. Finish cooking the sauce for 2 – 3 minutes and serve with boiled rice mixed with the sultanas and flaked almonds.

28

DUCK AUBRICHE   *Serves 4*

Marlowe's Restaurant's succulent way of serving duck with apricots.

Metric		lb/oz	U.S.A.
2 kg	Duck	4½ lb	4½ lb
100 g	Dried apricots	4 oz	1 cup
200 g	Breadcrumbs	8 oz	2 cups
1	Onion, chopped	1	1
2	Sage, chopped sprigs	2	2
3 tbsp	Apricot brandy	3 tbsp	4 tbsp
300 ml	Demi-glace sauce (see p. 16)	½ pt	1 cup

1. Soak the apricots in cold water for about 8 hours. Simmer them for a few minutes until soft.
2. Chop half the apricots and purée the other half.
3. To make the stuffing, combine the breadcrumbs, onion, sage and chopped apricots, and add a little of the apricot brandy to moisten.
4. Spoon the stuffing into the duck, rub it all over with salt and pepper, and place on a wire rack in a roasting tin.
5. Cover with foil and roast at 190°C, 375°F, Gas Mark 5 for 1 hour. Remove the foil and roast for a further 30 minutes.
6. Add the puréed apricots and the rest of the apricot brandy to the demi-glace sauce in a saucepan and heat gently. Pour a little over the roast duck, and serve the rest separately.

"Mine eyes smell onions; I shall weep anon"
          ALL'S WELL THAT ENDS WELL V. iii. 325.

GUINEA FOWL IN BURGUNDY AND PRUNE SAUCE   *Serves 6*

A rich and unusual dish from the Arden Hotel.

Metric		lb/oz	U.S.A.
	3 guinea fowl		
1 kg	each weighing	1½-2 lb	1½-2 lb
100 g	Oil	4 oz	½ cup
1	Medium onion, chopped	1	1
2	Garlic cloves, crushed	2	2
100 g	Flour	4 oz	1 cup
600 ml	Burgundy	1 pt	2½ cups
600 ml	Stock	1 pt	2½ cups
1	Prunes, large can	1	1

1. With a sharp knife split each fowl in half along the backbone.
2. Heat half the oil and fry the fowls quickly to seal the meat. Remove from the pan and place in an ovenproof casserole dish.

MARY ARDEN'S HOUSE

Before her marriage to John Shakespeare, William's mother lived in this farmhouse at Wilmcote, a picturesque village four miles from Stratford. The house's stone was quarried in the village and its oak timbers came from the nearby Forest of Arden, the Celtic name for a woodland place.

3. Put the remainder of the oil in the pan and fry the onion and the garlic until transparent but not browned.
4. Add the flour to the onions and stir well. Cook for a minute or two.
5. Slowly add the Burgundy and the stock, stirring all the time. Bring to the boil then pour over the guinea fowl. Season to taste.
6. Add the prunes and their juice to the casserole.
7. Place in a moderate oven, 180°C, 350°F, Gas Mark 4 for 2 hours.
8. Taste the sauce. If you would prefer it sweeter, add brown sugar to taste just before serving.

"Let me see, what I am to buy for our sheep-shearing feast? Three pound of sugar...four pound of prunes, and as many of raisins o' the sun."   THE WINTER'S TALE IV.iii.

Theatrical Stratford

Stratford has been attracting visitors since 1623 with the publication of the first folio of Shakespeare's plays, but it was not until the Jubilee in 1769 that visitors grew to large numbers, and not until the nineteenth century that a permanent Memorial Theatre was built.

What of the theatre in Shakespeare's own lifetime? Groups of strolling players performed at the Guild Hall and it is likely that the young William saw his first plays here, because in 1568, when Shakespeare would have been five years old, his father was elected Bailiff. As such, he was responsible for approving plays and collecting money from the players. Not all plays were considered acceptable, however, and on one occasion a company was paid six shillings *not* to perform!

Travelling players continued to visit the town and in 1746 John Ward's company performed at the old Town Hall for a summer season, with the proviso that five guineas be given to the poor. David Garrick came to Stratford in 1769 and organised Jubilee celebrations. A temporary theatre was erected in Bancroft Gardens, but the Garrick Jubilee was chiefly remarkable for not staging any Shakespeare at all!

In 1827 a theatre was built in Chapel Lane. It lasted nearly half a century and closed with a production of Hamlet. In 1879 the Memorial Theatre, based on the design of Shakespeare's Globe in London, was completed. Here, all Shakespeare's plays — except Titus Andronicus — were produced by Sir Frank Benson. A fire destroyed the theatre in 1926 and six years later the present Royal Shakespeare Theatre replaced it. Today, the theatre draws visitors from all over the world.

FILLETS OF PORK SAN ANTON   *Serves 4*

A colourful contribution from the chef of the Royal Shakespeare Theatre.

Metric		lb/oz	U.S.A.
	4 Pork fillets		
30 g	Flour	1 oz	¼ cup
30 g	Butter	1 oz	2 tbsp
50 g	Sweetcorn	2 oz	¾ cup
50 g	Red pepper, chopped	2 oz	¾ cup
50 g	Green pepper, chopped	2 oz	¾ cup
50 g	Onions, chopped	2 oz	¾ cup
50 g	Mushrooms, chopped	2 oz	¾ cup
1	Measure of brandy	1	1
150 g	Demi-glace sauce (see p.16)	¼ pt	½ cup
2 tbsp	Cream	2 tbsp	3 tbsp
30 g	Parsley, chopped	1 oz	2 tbsp

1. Trim and cut the pork into round "medallions" and then lightly flour both sides.
2. Heat the butter in the pan and sauté the pork to a golden brown.
3. Add the sweetcorn, peppers, onions and mushrooms to the pork and cook gently until tender.
4. Add the brandy to the pork and flame it to ensure the flavour is incorporated.
5. Now add the demi-glace or brown sauce to the mixture. Cook for 5 minutes to reduce the sauce.
6. Add the cream, chopped parsley and season to taste.
7. Place in serving dish and serve with rice and mixed salad.

ROYAL SHAKESPEARE THEATRE

Designed by Elizabeth Scott, the theatre opened in 1932 replacing the one that had been destroyed by fire.

FILLETS BEWICK   *Serves 4*

A mouthwatering dish from the Swan's Nest Hotel.

Metric		lb/oz	U.S.A.
	4 pork fillets (or veal escalopes)		
2 tbsp	*Flour*	2 tbsp	3 tbsp
30 g	*Butter*	1 oz	2 tbsp
2 tbsp	*Peach brandy*	2 tbsp	3 tbsp
1 can	*Peach slices*	1 can	1 can
150 ml	*Double cream*	¼ pt	½ cup
50 g	*Hazelnuts, toasted*	2 oz	½ cup

1. Flatten the escalopes* and flour them all over.
2. Sauté in butter. Remove escalopes when cooked and place on a warm serving dish.
3. Add peach brandy to pan juices and flame.
4. Add sliced peaches and cream, and boil to reduce, stirring continuously. Pour the sauce over the escalopes and decorate with toasted hazelnuts.

If you do not have a wooden meat mallet, you can use a rolling pin.

MEDAILLONS DE BOEUF GOURMETS   *Serves 4*

An all-time favourite at the Buccaneer restaurant.

Metric		lb/oz	U.S.A.
4	*175 g (6 oz) fillet steaks*	4	4
50 g	*Pâté*	2 oz	¼ cup
1	*Egg, beaten*	1	1
3 tbsp	*Breadcrumbs*	3 tbsp	4 tbsp
2 tbsp	*Oil for frying*	2 tbsp	2 tbsp
150 ml	*Madeira wine*	¼ pt	½ cup
50 g	*Mushrooms*	2 oz	8
300 ml	*Demi-glace sauce (see p.16)*	¼ pt	½ cup
1 tbsp	*Parsley, chopped*	1 tbsp	2 tbsp

1. Using a sharp knife, split each steak in half. Split again, taking the cut half-way through to make an envelope.
2. Divide the pâté equally and stuff the envelopes. Press down around the edges to seal. Season well.
3. Brush with beaten egg and coat with breadcrumbs.
4. Fry in a little oil until the steaks are cooked to your liking.
5. Remove the steaks from the pan and place on a serving dish to keep warm.
6. Pour the Madeira into the pan and add the mushrooms and demi-glace. Cook the mushrooms until the liquid has reduced by half. Season to taste.
7. Place the mushrooms on top of the steaks and pour over the sauce. Garnish with chopped parsley.

FIRST MEMORIAL THEATRE

The present theatre's Victorian predecessor owed its existence to the brewer, Charles Flower — whose product visitors can still enjoy in Stratford. Not everyone approved of the old building: on hearing that it had burnt down, the playwright George Bernard Shaw sent a telegram which simply said, "Congratulations"!

TOURNEDOS OLDE ENGLAND   *Serves 4*

Mead, an Old English honey liqueur, is used in this special occasion dish from the White Swan Hotel.

Metric		lb/oz	U.S.A.
4	*200 g (7 oz) tournedos*	4	4
90 g	*Butter*	3 oz	6 tbsp
30 g	*Flour*	1 oz	¼ cup
300 ml	*Stock*	½ pt	1 cup
2 tbsp	*Old English mead*	2 tbsp	3 tbsp
150 ml	*Cream*	¼ pt	½ cup
1 tsp	*Thyme*	1 tsp	1 tsp
	Freshly ground pepper		
250 g	*Mushrooms, sliced*	8 oz	2 cups
4	*Slices of bread*	4	4
2 tbsp	*Oil for frying*	2 tbsp	3 tbsp

1. Melt a third of the butter over a very gentle heat and stir in the flour.
2. Add the hot stock slowly, stirring all the time until the butter and flour are all mixed in.
3. Add the mead, cream, thyme, pepper and a pinch of salt. Heat gently but do not boil.
4. Sauté the mushrooms gently in the remainder of the butter. Season to taste and add to the sauce.
5. Cut circles out of the slices of bread and fry in oil until nicely brown. Drain and place on a warm serving dish.
6. Place the tournedos in the pan, adding a little more butter if required, season with salt and pepper and sauté for a few minutes until they are cooked to your liking.
7. Place a tournedos in the centre of each croûton and pour a little of the sauce over. Serve the remainder of the sauce separately.

36

THE GARRICK INN AND HARVARD HOUSE

Rebuilt after a fire in 1595, both the Garrick Inn and Harvard House would have been new houses when Shakespeare returned to Stratford, by this time rich and famous. Harvard House was then occupied by Thomas and Alice Rogers (you can see their initials carved beneath the front window), parents of Katherine Harvard whose son John founded Harvard University in the USA by leaving a legacy of £779 17s 2d — less than $2,000!

The Inn was not licensed until the early 1700s. Originally called The Reindeer, it was renamed after the actor David Garrick.

(Transatlantic visitors may also like to know that the American fountain, at the top of Rother Street, was presented to the town by George W. Childs of Philadelphia in Queen Victoria's Golden Jubilee year, when it was unveiled by Henry Irving.)

FALCON GREEN PEPPER STEAK   *Serves 4*

This rich flambéed steak recipe comes from the chef of the Falcon Hotel.

Metric		lb/oz	U.S.A.
	4 sirloin steaks		
50 g	Butter	2 oz	¼ cup
½	Stick of celery, chopped	½	½
1	Onion, sliced	1	1
15 g	Black peppercorns, crushed	½ oz	2 tbsp
2	Green peppers, thinly sliced	2	2
1	Measure of brandy	1	1
150 ml	Demi-glace sauce (see p.16)	¼ pt	½ cup
30 ml	Red wine	2 tbsp	3 tbsp
75 ml	Cream	⅛ pt	¼ cup

1. Sauté the steaks in the butter to seal, add the celery, onion, peppercorns and green pepper.
2. Pour over the brandy and flame.
3. Add demi-glace or brown sauce, and red wine. Cook slowly until the vegetables are tender and the steaks are cooked.
4. Place the steaks on a heated serving dish.
5. Add the cream to the sauce and heat gently but do not boil.
6. Pour a little of the sauce over the steaks and serve the rest separately.

Spot the amusing Victorian maids' bells in the Falcon Hotel. (Speak nicely to the porter if you are staying there and he may even show you how they play a tune!)

As you like it

FILET DE BOEUF A LA FICELLE   *Serves 8*

A lovely way to achieve a light and tasty beef. This recipe comes from the Welcombe Hotel.

Metric		lb/oz	U.S.A.
2 kg	Fillet of beef	4 lb	4 lb
600 ml	Beef stock	1 pt	2½ cups
1	Onion, large chopped	1	1
5	Cloves	5	5
2	Celery hearts, chopped	2	2
1	Fresh parsley, bunch	1	1
1	Fresh tarragon, bunch	1	1
1 tsp	Coarse salt	1 tsp	1 tsp
½ tsp	White peppercorns	½ tsp	½ tsp
2	Marrow bones	2	2
500 g	Carrots, chopped	1 lb	1 lb
250 g	Swede, chopped	½ lb	½ lb
500 g	Courgettes, chopped	1 lb	1 lb
500 g	Leeks, chopped	1 lb	1 lb
500 g	Button onions	1 lb	1 lb
750 g	Potatoes	1½ lb	1½ lb
	Horseradish sauce, mixed with whipped cream		

1. Place the beef stock in a large saucepan. Stick the cloves into the onion and add it to the stock, with the celery, parsley, tarragon, salt and peppercorns. Bring the liquid to the boil. Skim the top of the liquid, turn down the heat and simmer gently.
2. Put the marrow bones and a selection of the vegetables, except the potatoes, into the stock, leaving room for the fillet. Cook the potatoes and any vegetables which will not fit into the meat pot separately.
3. Trim the fillet of beef and tie string round it at the thicker end.
4. Put the fillet into the boiling stock, tying the end of the string to the handle of the pan. Cook the fillet for about 50 minutes. It must be kept pink.
5. Remove the beef when it is cooked and place in the centre of a warm serving dish; arrange the vegetables round the edge, alternating the colours.
6. Serve with horseradish sauce, mixed with whipped cream, and offer gherkins and coarse salt separately.

Theodore Roosevelt, President of the United States (and honoured by millions of children whose teddy bears are named after him!), stayed in the house which is now the Welcombe Hotel as a guest of his friend Sir George Otto Trevelyan, historian of the American Revolution.

KIDNEYS IN RED WINE
ROGNONS D'AGNEAU MARCHAND DE VINS   *Serves 4*

A delicious kidney dish from the Grosvenor House Hotel.

Metric		lb/oz	U.S.A.
500 g	Lambs' kidneys, cored, skinned, thinly sliced	1 lb	1 lb
50 g	Butter	2 oz	¼ cup
1	Onion, finely diced	1	1
2	Garlic cloves, crushed	2	2
100 g	Lean bacon, chopped	4 oz	4 oz
100 g	Mushrooms, sliced	4 oz	1 cup
150 ml	Red wine	¼ pt	½ cup
150 ml	Espagnole sauce (see p.16)	¼ pt	½ cup
4	Tomatoes, blanched and sliced	4	4

1. Melt the butter in a frying pan and fry the onion with the garlic and bacon until transparent.
2. Add kidneys and mushrooms. Simmer for five minutes.
3. Pour in the red wine, espagnole sauce and sliced tomato and simmer for five minutes. Serve on a bed of rice.

STEAK, KIDNEY AND OYSTER PIE   *Serves 6*

An English dish older than Shakespeare! This recipe comes from the Alveston Manor Hotel—first home of Titania and still a setting fit for a queen!

Metric		lb/oz	U.S.A.
1 kg	Topside of beef, cubed	2 lb	2 lb
2 tbsp	Oil	2 tbsp	3 tbsp
100 g	Onion, finely chopped	4 oz	1 cup
2	Bay leaves	2	2
600 g	Lambs' kidneys, cubed	1¼ lb	1¼ lb
150 ml	Red wine	¼ pt	½ cup
50 g	Flour	2 oz	¼ cup
750 ml	Brown stock	1½ pt	3 cups
1 tbsp	Tomato purée	1 tbsp	1 tbsp
6	Oysters	6	6
500 g	Puff pastry	1 lb	1 lb
1	Egg, beaten	1	1

1. Melt the oil gently in a frying pan and sauté the beef lightly with the onion and the bay leaves.
2. Add the cubed kidney and pour over the red wine.

The first performance of "A Midsummer Night's Dream" was probably held on the Cedar Lawn at Alveston Manor. In fact, the play's stage directions correspond to the hotel's garden before it was redesigned in the 19th century. More recent productions have been staged on the lawn by Oxford and Cambridge universities.

3. When all the meat is sealed add the flour to thicken, stirring all the time. Gradually add the stock and tomato purée, season to taste and gently simmer until tender (1½-2 hours).
4. Add the oysters at the last minute to preserve the flavour.
5. Place the filling into a pie dish and cover with pastry. Decorate with pastry "leaves" and brush with beaten egg. Cook at 200°C, 400°F, Gas Mark 6, for 30 minutes.

"Why, then the world's mine oyster, which I with sword will open".   *THE MERRY WIVES OF WINDSOR. II. ii. 2.*

BRAISED OXTAILS   *Serves 6*

A speciality of the Dirty Duck Restaurant.

Metric		lb/oz	U.S.A.
	2 oxtails		
2 tbsp	Seasoned flour	2 tbsp	3 tbsp
50 g	Beef dripping	2 oz	¼ cup
2	Onions, sliced	2	2
½ bott	Dry red wine	½ bott	½ bott
450 ml	Beef stock	¾ pt	1½ cups
1	Bouquet garni	1	1
2	Bay leaves	2	2
1 tbsp	Redcurrant jelly	1 tbsp	1 tbsp
375 g	Carrots, sliced	12 oz	3 cups
2	Small turnips, sliced	2	2
1 tbsp	Lemon juice	1 tbsp	1 tbsp
1 tbsp	Tomato purée	1 tbsp	1 tbsp
175 g	Mushrooms	6 oz	6 oz

1. Chop oxtails into 5 cm (2") lengths and coat lightly in seasoned flour.
2. Fry in fat for five minutes and then transfer them to a large metal ovenproof casserole or saucepan.
3. Fry the onions in the same fat until starting to colour. Add to oxtail.
4. Pour wine and beef stock over the oxtail and onions and bring to the boil.
5. Add salt, pepper, bouquet garni, bay leaves and redcurrant jelly and simmer for 2 hours.
6. Strain liquid off into a bowl. When cool, remove fat from the liquid. Put meat and vegetables into an ovenproof casserole.
7. Pour the liquid over the oxtails, add carrots and turnips, lemon juice and tomato purée and bring to the boil.
8. Place in the oven, 180°C, 350°F, Gas Mark 4 and cook for 1 hour.
9. Add mushrooms for the last ten minutes.

"My friends were poor but honest."
                        ALL'S WELL THAT ENDS WELL I.iii.203

ANN HATHAWAY'S COTTAGE

Anne Hathaway lived in this house at Shottery with her family until her marriage to William Shakespeare. Because generations of Hathaways lived in the house in an unbroken line from 1490 until 1892, it provides an exceptional example of a typical yeoman's house of the Elizabethan period. (Indeed, the carved oak bed has not been out of the room where it is now displayed for 400 years.)

CAULIFLOWER ROYALE   *Serves 8*

Metric		*lb/oz*	*U.S.A.*
1	*Cauliflower, large*	1	1
50 g	*Mushrooms, sliced*	2 oz	¾ cup
50 g	*Cheese, grated*	2 oz	2 oz
5	*Eggs*	5	5
900 ml	*Milk*	1½ pts	3 cups

1. Cut the cauliflower into florets and place in a buttered baking dish. Season with salt and pepper.
2. Place the mushrooms on top of the cauliflower and sprinkle with the cheese.
3. Whisk the eggs and milk together and pour over the cauliflower.
4. Bake in a pre-heated oven at 125°C, 250°F, Gas Mark 1 for approximately one hour.

A cottage garden recipe from the Grosvenor House Hotel.

CABBAGE CREAMS *Serves 8*

This unusual vegetable recipe was provided by the chef of the Grosvenor House Hotel — a lovely little hotel run by a mother and her four daughters.

Metric		lb/oz	U.S.A.
1 kg	Cabbage	2 lb	2 lb
20 g	Butter	½ oz	1 tbsp
300 ml	Béchamel sauce	½ pt	1 cup
2	Eggs	2	2
1	Nutmeg, pinch of	1	1
	8 Dariole moulds or small ramekins		

1. Blanch cabbage, drain and press between two plates to remove the excess water. Use leaves to line the buttered moulds, and purée the remaining cabbage in a liquidiser.
2. Melt the butter, cook slowly to a nut brown, add the cabbage purée and stir over the heat until dry.
3. Add the béchamel sauce and mix well.
4. Remove from the heat, beat in the eggs, season well and add the nutmeg.
5. Spoon the mixture into prepared moulds, cover with foil and cook in a bain-marie (a baking tin containing hot water) in the oven, pre-heated to 180°C, 350°F, Gas Mark 4 for 15 – 20 minutes.

Béchamel sauce

Metric		lb/oz	U.S.A.
300 ml	Milk	½ pt	1¼ cups
1	Small onion, chopped	1	1
1	Carrot, chopped	1	1
1	Stick of celery, chopped	1	1
1	Bay leaf	1	1
1	Clove	1	1
½ tsp	Mace, ground	½ tsp	½ tsp
2	Peppercorns	2	2
25 g	Butter	1 oz	2 tbsp
30 g	Flour	1½ oz	¼ cup

1. Place the milk and vegetables in a saucepan and bring slowly to the boil, then add the herbs and spices. Cover the pan with a tightly fitting lid.
2. Remove the saucepan from the heat and leave covered for half an hour to infuse.
3. Strain off the milk and remove the vegetables from the pan.
4. Melt the butter in the pan slowly, add the flour and cook for a few minutes, stirring all the time. Be careful not to brown the mixture.
5. Stir the flavoured milk gradually into the flour until the mixture is smooth.
6. Bring the sauce to the boil, stirring all the time.

THE GOWER MEMORIAL: a detail is shown above right.

Desserts and Teatime Treats

STRATFORD SYLLABUB

Serves 4

An easy but wickedly delicious dessert from the Swan's Nest Hotel.

Metric		lb/oz	U.S.A.
300 ml	*Double cream*	½ pt	1 cup
1	*Lemon, grated rind and juice*	1	1
	Brandy (As you like it!)		
1 tsp	*Nutmeg, grated*	1 tsp	1 tsp

1. Whisk the cream to form peaks. During whisking, slowly add lemon juice and rind, and brandy to taste.
2. Transfer to sundae dishes, sprinkle with nutmeg and serve chilled.

AMBER TART

Serves 6

A melt-in-the-mouth creation which can be served hot as a dessert or cold for tea, this recipe comes from the Hathaway Tea Rooms in the High Street.

Metric		lb/oz	U.S.A.
250 g	*Shortcrust pastry*	8 oz	8 oz
30 g	*Softened butter*	1 oz	2 tbsp
50 g	*Caster sugar*	2 oz	4 tbsp
2 tbsp	*Chunky marmalade*	2 tbsp	2 tbsp
2	*Eggs*	2	2
1 tbsp	*Cream*	1 tbsp	1 tbsp

1. Line a 20 cm (8") greased flan tin with pastry.
2. Beat the butter and sugar together until light and creamy. Add the marmalade and eggs, mix well. Stir in the cream.
3. Pour into the flan tin and bake in a moderate oven, 190°C, 375°F, Gas Mark 5, for 30 – 35 minutes.

HOME-MADE LIQUEUR ICE-CREAM *Makes about 1 gallon*

A perfect ending from the marvellous Buccaneer Restaurant.

Metric		lb/oz	U.S.A.
10	*Eggs*	10	10
100 g	*Caster sugar*	4 oz	½ cup
450 ml	*Double cream*	¾ pt	1½ cups
2 tbsp	*Liqueur*	2 tbsp	3 tbsp

1. Separate the egg yolks from the whites and place in two mixing bowls.
2. Beat the egg yolks and the sugar until white and creamy. Continue whisking until doubled in volume.
3. Whip the cream until it just holds its shape.
4. Whisk the egg whites until stiff and standing in peaks.
5. Fold the egg yolk mixture and the whipped cream gently into the egg white using a metal spoon. Be careful not to beat the mixture or you will lose the volume.
6. Stir in the liqueur of your choice or halve the mixture and make two varieties.
7. Pour into a 5 litre or gallon plastic container and freeze.

"When icicles hang by the wall/ And Dick the shepherd blows his nail,/ And Tom bears logs into the hall/ And milk comes frozen home in pail." LOVE'S LABOUR'S LOST V.ii.920

CLOPTON BRIDGE

This bridge was carrying traffic across the River Avon into Stratford when Columbus sailed the Atlantic. It continues to do so today. Named after Sir Hugh Clopton, the fourteen-arched stone bridge replaced a wooden structure that, according to contemporary accounts, caused people to think twice before coming to Stratford when the river was high.

PUCK'S POTION   *Serves 4 – 6*

A magical concoction with which to make friends and influence people!

Metric		lb/oz	U.S.A.
4	Eggs, separated	4	4
1 pkt	Gelatine	1 pkt	1pkt
4 tbsp	Golden syrup	4 tbsp	5 tbsp
1	Lemon, rind and juice	1	1
450 ml	Whipping cream	¾ pt	1 ½ cups

1. Whip the egg whites very stiffly.
2. Melt the gelatine in a little water, heating gently and stirring continuously.
3. Add 3 tbsp golden syrup to the gelatine mixture and fold gently into the egg white.
4. Spoon the mixture into a well greased soufflé dish and refrigerate until set. Unmould and serve with syrup sauce.
5. To make the syrup sauce, beat the egg yolks until creamy then mix in 1 tbsp syrup and the lemon juice and rind.
6. Whip the cream until it holds its shape but is not too thick, then stir in the egg mixture. Transfer to a serving dish and chill before serving.

"Sweets to the sweet."   HAMLET V.i.265.

PINEAPPLE REGENCE   *Serves 4*

A regal offering from the White Swan Hotel.

Metric		lb/oz	U.S.A.
1	Fresh pineapple	1	1
	Sugar to taste		
	Kirsch (As you like it!)		
300 ml	Double cream	½ pt	1 cup

1. Cut the top and bottom off the pineapple, and also cut around the inside of the skin, leaving it whole and taking out the fruit. Keep the top.
2. Cut the fruit into 2 cm (½") cubes, place in a bowl and sprinkle with sugar. Pour over the kirsch and leave for a few hours to marinate.
3. Whip the cream until it is stiff and add to the pineapple and kirsch.
4. Stand the pineapple shell on a serving dish, put the mixture inside the shell until full. Place the top back on the pineapple and serve.

"A morsel for a monarch."
                              ANTONY AND CLEOPATRA I.v.31

WARWICKSHIRE PUDDING   *Serves 6*

"Our WARWICKSHIRE the heart of England is,
As you must evidently have prov'd by this:
Having it with more spirit dignified,
Than all our English Counties are beside."
(Reference to Shakespeare by Sir Aston Cokain in 1658)

Metric		lb/oz	U.S.A.
2	Eggs	2	2
300 ml	Milk	½ pt	1 cup
250 g	Flour	8 oz	2 cups
100 g	Butter	4 oz	½ cup
100 g	Sugar	4 oz	½ cup
250 g	Raspberry or apricot jam	½ lb	¾ cup

1. Beat the eggs and stir in the milk.
2. Sift the flour and rub in the butter until it resembles fine breadcrumbs, then stir in the sugar.
3. Add the egg mixture gradually, beating until you have a smooth batter.
4. Grease a pudding basin and spoon the jam into the bottom.
5. Pour the batter on top and cover tightly with a pudding cloth.
6. Place in a steamer or a large covered saucepan of boiling water and steam for 1½ hours. Top up the water if necessary during cooking.

BAKED CHEESECAKE   *Serves 6 – 8*

From the pastry chef of the Cobweb Tea Rooms.

Metric		lb/oz	U.S.A.
	For the pastry:		
250 g	Flour	8 oz	2 cups
50 g	Butter	2 oz	¼ cup
50 g	Lard	2 oz	¼ cup
50 g	Caster sugar	2 oz	4 tbsp
1	Egg, beaten	1	1
	For the cheese filling:		
4	Eggs	4	4
175 g	Caster sugar	6 oz	¾ cup
600 g	Curd or soft cream cheese	1 ¼ lb	1 ¼ lb
150 ml	Milk	4 oz	½ cup
1	Lemon, grated rind	1	1
50 g	Sultanas	2 oz	¼ cup
1 – 2	Vanilla essence drops	1 – 2	1 – 2
50 g	Melted butter	2 oz	¼ cup
175 g	Plain flour	6 oz	1 ½ cups
2 tbsp	Icing sugar	2 tbsp	3 tbsp
75 ml	Whipping cream	2 oz	¼ cup

1. Put the flour into a bowl with a pinch of salt and rub in the fats until the mixture resembles fine breadcrumbs.
2. Stir in the caster sugar and the beaten egg and mix to a soft dough.
3. Roll out the pastry on a floured board and line a greased 25 cm (10") flan tin.
4. To make the filling, beat the eggs and sugar until stiff.
5. Mix the cheese, milk, lemon rind, sultanas, essence and a pinch of salt until smooth. Beat in the melted butter.
6. Finally, fold in the beaten eggs and the flour.
7. Put the mixture into the prepared baking tin and bake slowly at 180°C, 350°F, Gas Mark 4 for 40 minutes until golden brown. Allow to cool.
8. Dust with icing sugar and serve with whipped cream.

"Good sooth, she is/The queen of curds and cream."
THE WINTER'S TALE IV. iii. 160

RED ROSE PLUM PIE

"Shall I compare thee to a summer's day?
Thou art more lovely and more temperate."

To add a fragrant flavour to plum or damson pie, sprinkle a handful of red rose petals over the fruit before topping with pastry.

STRAWBERRY AND PORTYNGGALE* SHORTCAKE

*My Lord of Ely, when I was last in Holborn,
I saw good strawberries in your garden there".*

RICHARD III III.iv.31.

Metric		lb/oz	U.S.A.
500 g	Strawberries	1 lb	1 lb
275 g	Flour	9 oz	2¼ cups
125 g	Butter	5 oz	⅔ cup
30 g	Lard	1 oz	2 tbsp
1	Orange, finely grated rind and juice	1	1
75 g	Icing sugar	3 oz	⅓ cup
1 pkt	Red quick jel	1 pkt	1 pkt
2 tbsp	Orange liqueur	2 tbsp	2 tbsp
150 ml	Cream	¼ pt	½ cup

1. Wash, hull and drain the strawberries. Pre-heat the oven to 180°C, 350°F, Gas Mark 4.
2. Sift the flour with a generous pinch of salt and rub in the butter and lard until the mixture resembles fine breadcrumbs. Add the finely grated rind and a little juice.
3. Sift in the icing sugar and add to the mixture. Knead to a dough, then chill thoroughly.
4. Sprinkle a little icing sugar onto the table or a board and onto the rolling pin and roll out the shortcake.
5. Put into a greased straightsided sandwich tin and press down with the fingers, easing the mixture into the sides. Cook for 20 – 25 minutes until light golden brown.
6. Make a glaze with the quick jel, following the instructions on the packet but substituting a tablespoonful of liqueur for the same amount of water and brush the top of the shortcake whilst still hot.
7. Arrange the strawberries on top and cover with the glaze. Whip the cream until thick then add 1 tbsp liqueur and re-whip. Pipe around the edge of the shortcake.

* In Shakespearian times, oranges were sometimes called portynggales, a reference to Portuguese oranges.

HALL'S CROFT

Hall's Croft was the home of Shakespeare's elder daughter, Susanna, and her husband Dr John Hall, who had a medical practice in the town. Visitors can see Dr Hall's dispensary, complete with apothecaries' jars, pestles and mortars, herbs and surgical instruments of the day, together with an outstanding collection of Elizabethan furniture. This view shows the earlier, 16th century part of the house; 17th century additions at the front were probably made by Dr Hall.

CHARLOTTE AU CHOCOLAT   *Serves 6-8*

A light chocolate confection from the Marianne Restaurant.

Metric		lb/oz	U.S.A.
125 g	*Butter*	5 oz	⅔ cup
2 tbsp	*Caster sugar*	2 tbsp	2 tbsp
16	*Sponge fingers*	16	16
250 g	*Cooking chocolate*	8 oz	8 oz
6	*Egg yolks*	6	6
10	*Egg whites*	10	10

1. Grease a large bowl with a little of the butter and sprinkle sugar inside the bowl. Line it with sponge fingers.
2. In a double saucepan, warm the chocolate and the rest of the butter. When both have melted, add the egg yolks and stir them into the mixture.
3. Beat the egg whites until stiff and fold into the chocolate mixture. Pour into the prepared bowl.
4. Put the bowl into the freezer or refrigerator and, when cold, turn out on to a plate.
5. To serve, pour over a little melted chocolate or, more simply, sprinkle grated chocolate or vermicelli on top.

"'Tis an ill cook that cannot lick his own fingers."
                    ROMEO AND JULIET IV.ii.6

LEMON CHEESE TORTEN   *Serves 8 – 10*

A rich dessert/cake from the Shakespeare Hotel.

Metric		lb/oz	U.S.A.
1	*20 cm (8″) plain sponge cake*	1	1
30 g	*Gelatine*	1 oz	1 pkt
250 g	*Cottage or cream cheese*	½ lb	½ lb
175 g	*Lemon curd*	6 oz	½ cup
30 g	*Caster sugar*	1 oz	2 tbsp
300 ml	*Whipping cream*	½ pt	1 cup
50 g	*Sultanas*	2 oz	¼ cup
1 tbsp	*Icing sugar, sieved*	1 tbsp	1tbsp

1. Slice the sponge cake in half and place the bottom half into a flan ring or loose-bottomed cake tin lined with a 5 cm (2½″) greaseproof paper collar.
2. Soak the gelatine in a little water and dissolve over a low heat.
3. Mix together the cheese, lemon curd and sugar.
4. Add the gelatine and fold in whipped cream and sultanas.
5. Pour the mixture into the prepared flan ring and refrigerate.
6. When set, gently ease out of the tin and place on a serving plate. Place the remaining half of sponge on top of the cheese mixture and dust with icing sugar.

MERRY CAKE

This recipe and the one following are delicious Hathaway Tea Rooms specialities.

Metric		lb/oz	U.S.A.
250 g	Shortcrust pastry	8 oz	8 oz
2 tbsp	Raspberry jam	2 tbsp	3tbsp
50 g	Butter	2 oz	¼ cup
50 g	Caster sugar	2 oz	¼ cup
1	Egg	1	1
4 tbsp	Sultanas	4 tbsp	5 tbsp
1 tbsp	Walnuts, chopped	1 tbsp	1 tbsp
1 tbsp	Glacé cherries	1 tbsp	1 tbsp
1 tbsp	Ground rice	1 tbsp	1 tbsp
1 tbsp	Ground almonds	1 tbsp	1 tbsp
1 tbsp	Sherry (optional)	1 tbsp	1 tbsp

1. Line a 20 cm (8") greased flan tin with shortcrust pastry.
2. Spread the raspberry jam over the pastry.
3. Cream together the butter and sugar. Beat in the egg.
4. Add the sultanas, walnuts, glacé cherries, ground rice and ground almonds. Stir in the sherry.
5. Pour the mixture into the flan case and bake in a moderate oven, 180°C, 350°F, Gas Mark 4, for 30 – 35 minutes or until lightly brown.

APRICOT EGGS

Metric		lb/oz	U.S.A.
100 g	Butter	4 oz	½ cup
100 g	Caster sugar	4 oz	½ cup
2	Eggs	2	2
100 g	Self-raising flour	4 oz	¾ cup
1	Apricots, large can	1	1
300 ml	Double cream	½ pt	1 cup

1. Beat the butter and sugar together until light and creamy.
2. Whisk in the eggs one at a time, adding a little flour between each egg.
3. Fold in the remaining flour. Pour into a greased and lined Swiss roll tin.
4. Bake in a pre-heated oven, 180°C, 350°F, Gas Mark 4, for 20 – 25 minutes.
5. Allow to cool in the tin then turn out.
6. Cut out rounds of cake slightly larger than apricot halves. Moisten the rounds with the juice from the tin of apricots.
7. Place an apricot half on each sponge cake and pipe a ring of whipped cream round each to represent egg white.

MEASURE FOR MEASURE CARROT CAKE

Until you've tried it you will never believe how delicious carrot cake can be. This old recipe is very easy to follow—just measure all the major ingredients in the same cup.

Metric		lb/oz	U.S.A.
2 cups	Flour	2 cups	2 cups
2 cups	Caster sugar	2 cups	2 cups
2 tsp	Mixed spice	2 tsp	2 tsp
2 tsp	Baking powder	2 tsp	2 tsp
¾ cup	Oil	¾ cup	¾ cup
3	Eggs	3	3
3 cups	Carrots, grated	3 cups	3 cups
½ cup	Nuts, chopped	½ cup	½ cup
1 cup	Raisins	1 cup	1 cup
	For the icing:		
¼ cup	Butter	¼ cup	¼ cup
2 cups	Icing sugar	2 cups	2 cups
1 tsp	Vanilla essence	1 tsp	1 tsp

1. Mix together the flour, caster sugar, mixed spice, and baking powder. Add a teaspoonful of salt.
2. Beat in the oil until you have a smooth batter.
3. Lightly whisk the eggs and add slowly to the batter beating all the time.

4. Fold in the carrot, nuts and raisins.
5. Turn into a greased 20 cm (8") cake tin and bake in a moderate oven at 180°C, 350°F, Gas Mark 4 for 1 ¼ hours. Leave in the tin for 10 minutes before cooling on a wire tray.
6. To make the icing, beat together the butter and icing sugar until light and creamy. Add the vanilla essence. Smooth over the top of the cake.

COVENTRY CAKES   *Makes 12*

Coventry cakes are triangular. The three corners were said to represent the Trinity.

Metric		lb/oz	U.S.A.
100 g	Butter	4 oz	½ cup
50 g	Caster sugar	2 oz	4 tbsp
250 g	Currants	8 oz	1 ¼ cups
100g	Mixed peel	4 oz	⅔ cup
2 tsp	Mixed spices	2 tsp	2 tsp
500 g	Puff pastry	1 lb	1 lb
2 tbsp	Granulated sugar for topping	2 tbsp	2 tbsp
	Milk for glaze		

1. To make the filling, cream the butter and sugar until light and fluffy, then stir in the currants, peel and spices.
2. Roll the pastry 3 mm (⅛") thick and cut into 10 cm (4") squares.
3. Spoon the filling into the centre of each one and brush the edges with cold water.
4. Fold corner-to-corner, and seal the edges firmly.
5. Using a sharp knife, cut a small X on top of each cake, then brush all over with milk.
6. Sprinkle liberally with granulated sugar, and bake at 200°C, 400°F, Gas Mark 6 for 20 – 25 minutes until puffy and golden.

Coventry is just 19 miles from Stratford. It is famous for its spectacular 20th century cathedral.

MASON'S COURT

Thatched roofs and half timbering led to many fires in Elizabethan times (Stratford suffered two major ones in 1594 and 5) so the survival of early 15th century Mason's Court in Rother Street is all the more remarkable. It shows, too, that home improvements are not just a modern phenomenon: the right-hand upper storey used to overhang the pavement like the one on the left, but in the 16th century the ground floor was pushed out.

Stratford's surrounding villages (or should we say hamlets!) merit a visit. This rhyme, mentioning some of them, is said to have been the result of an evening's carousing at Bidford in which Shakespeare took part:

> *"Piping Pebworth, Dancing Marston,*
> *Haunted Hillborough, Hungry Grafton,*
> *Dodging Exhall, Papist Wixford,*
> *Beggarly Broom, and Drunken Bidford."*

ENGLISH BREAD PUDDING

This is a very good way of using up your stale bread, no doubt popular in Hungry Grafton! Serve hot or cold.

Metric		lb/oz	U.S.A.
1	Bread, large loaf	1	1
175 g	Brown sugar	6 oz	¾ cup
400 g	Mixed dried fruit	12 oz	2 cups
2 tsp	Mixed spice	2 tsp	2 tsp
4 tbsp	Marmalade	4 tbsp	5 tbsp
125 g	Suet	5 oz	1 cup
50 g	Mixed chopped shelled nuts	2 oz	½ cup
3	Eggs	3	3
3 tbsp	Granulated sugar	3 tbsp	3 tbsp

1. Cover the bread with water and soak for 2 – 3 hours.
2. Pour off the water and squeeze out as much as possible.
3. Break up the bread into small pieces.
4. Stir in the brown sugar, mixed fruit, mixed spice, marmalade, suet, nuts and the beaten eggs.
5. Place in a well greased baking tin and bake in the centre of a moderate oven, 170°C, 325°F, Gas Mark 3, for about 1 hour until golden brown.
6. Remove from the oven and sprinkle with granulated sugar. Return to the oven for a further 10 minutes to crisp the top.

LEMON GERANIUM CAKE

A light sponge which owes its fragrance to the scented geranium leaves on which it is cooked.

Metric		lb/oz	U.S.A.
175 g	Butter	6 oz	1 cup
175 g	Sugar	6 oz	¾ cup
3	Eggs	3	3
175 g	Flour	6 oz	1½ cups
1 tsp	Baking powder	1 tsp	1 tsp
3 tbsp	Milk	3 tbsp	4 tbsp
4	Lemon-scented geranium leaves	4	4
	For the cream filling:		
50 g	Butter	2 oz	¼ cup
50 g	Sugar	2 oz	4 tbsp
1	Lemon, grated rind and juice	1	1

1. Warm the fat and sugar, then cream until light and fluffy.
2. Add the beaten eggs a little at a time, beating well.
3. Fold in the sieved flour and baking powder.
4. Add the milk and mix well.
5. Grease and line two 18 cm (7″) sandwich tins with oiled paper then place lemon geranium leaves neatly in the bottom of the tin.
6. Carefully spoon the mixture on to the leaves. Bake in a pre-heated oven at 180°C, 350°F, Gas Mark 4 for 25 – 30 minutes until golden brown.
7. Turn out on to a wire rack, carefully removing the leaves.
8. To make the cream filling, beat together the butter and sugar until fluffy. Add the rind and juice of the lemon, and continue beating for a few minutes until all the lemon juice is absorbed into the cream.
9. Sandwich the two sponge halves together with the cream in the middle. Dust with sugar if liked.

HOME-MADE COTTAGE CHEESE

Stratford lies in the very heart of England — a country famous for its tasty country cheeses. Even city dwellers can make this simple, light and lovely variety. The only special equipment needed is muslin (cheesecloth).

1. Don't throw away milk that's turned sour by being left out of the fridge. Transfer it to a basin, cover with a saucer and set on one side until the milk is thick.
2. Stir in a generous pinch of salt and transfer to a muslin bag (or square of muslin gathered up and tied firmly with string). Hang this over the sink or a bowl to drain for

NEW PLACE CORNER, CHAPEL STREET

Standing on the corner of Scholar's Lane by the Falcon Hotel you can see New Place Gardens, the site of Shakespeare's house. Next to it is Nash's House, owned by Thomas Nash who married Shakespeare's granddaughter Elizabeth Hall. The nine gables further along the street mark the Shakespeare Hotel. The first five gables date back to the early 1600s but the rest were rebuilt in 1920.

several hours, squeezing gently occasionally.

3. When the cheese has drained, transfer to a bowl and cover with a weighted saucer.
4. Refrigerate overnight, drain off any whey, and unmould.

Variations Mix chopped fresh herbs, or sweet peppers, or pineapple with the cheese before refrigerating.

HERB VINEGARS

"There's rosemary, that's for remembrance; pray you, love, remember: and there is pansies, that's for thoughts."
HAMLET IV.v.174.

Bottled herb vinegars look decorative and impart a delicious flavour when used in dressings and sauces. Rosemary, tarragon and thyme are all suitable for this use, and empty mixer drink bottles with screw tops are ideal for presenting these vinegars as gifts.

1. To make the vinegar, bruise a handful of the chosen fresh herbs with a wooden spoon and put into a large screw-top jar.
2. Bring white wine vinegar to the boil and pour over the leaves. Screw up the lid tightly and put in a dark cupboard for two weeks.
3. Ease a decorative sprig of the herb, head down, into the empty mixer drink bottle, strain the infused vinegar into a jug, and then pour carefully into the bottles. Seal tightly, and label.

SLOE GIN

The longer you wait, the better it gets— sloe, sloe, quick, quick, sloe!

Metric		lb/oz	U.S.A.
250 g	Sloes	½ lb	½ cup
75 g	Caster sugar	3 oz	⅓ cup
4	Shelled almonds or	4	4
2 drops	Almond essence	2 drops	2 drops
500 ml	Gin	1 pint	1 pint

1. Wash and dry the sloes and remove the stalks.
2. Prick each sloe thoroughly with a large needle and put into a jar with the sugar and almonds or almond essence. Pour over the gin.
3. Screw the lid on gently. Store in a dark cupboard for two to three months, shaking occasionally.
4. Strain through muslin and bottle.

Index

60

MEASURES & CONVERSIONS

Ingredients are given in metric. Imperial and American measures. **Use measures from one column only.**
Teaspoon and tablespoon measures in the metric column correspond to 5 ml and 15 ml respectively.
The table below will help our American readers.

English	**American**
Baking powder	Baking soda
Beetroots	Beets
Caster sugar	Fine granulated sugar
Chicory	Endive
Courgettes	Zucchini
Double cream	Heavy cream
Flaked almonds	Slivered almonds
Gherkins	Baby dill pickles
Glacé cherries	Candied red cherries
Golden syrup	Light corn syrup
Grill	Broil
Icing sugar	Confectioners' sugar
Lemon curd	Lemon cheese
Plain chocolate	Semi-sweet chocolate
Redcurrant jelly	Cranberry jelly
Single cream	Light cream
Spring onions	Scallions
Sultanas	Light raisins
Swedes	Rutabagas

RESTAURANTS & HOTELS

We would like to thank the following for their help and generosity in giving us the recipes listed below. Stratford telephone numbers and opening times are also provided.

ALVESTON MANOR HOTEL, Clopton Bridge   4581
Chef: K. Huddespith
   Steak, kidney and oyster pie, 38
Luncheon: 12.15-2 pm. Dinner: 6.15-9.30 pm
7-9.30 pm (Sun and when theatre is closed)

ARDEN HOTEL, Waterside   294949
Chef: Mr D. Tilley
   Guinea fowl in Burgundy and prune sauce, 28
Luncheon: 12.30-2 pm. Dinner: 6-9 pm

BOATHOUSE, Bridgefoot   295297
Chefs: Ruth Sainsbury and Briony Marriott
   Chicory and ham mornay, 18
Luncheon: 12-2.30 pm (7 days)
Dinner 7-10.30 pm (Sun-Mon).
7-midnight (Tues-Thur). 7-12.30 am (Fri-Sat)

BUCCANEER RESTAURANT, Warwick Road   292550
Chef: Paul Thor-Straten
   Champignons Languedocienne, 15
   Paupiettes de veau saumon fumé, 22
   Medaillons de boeuf gourmets, 32
   Home-made liqueur ice-cream, 44
Dinner: 7-11.30 pm (except Mon)

COBWEB TEA ROOMS, Sheep Street   293372
Chef: Roland Wanke
   Baked cheesecake, 47
Open: 9 am-6 pm (Mon-Sat). 3-6 pm (Sun)

THE DIRTY DUCK, Waterside   297312
Chef: Neil Haywood
   Braised oxtails, 39
Luncheon: 12-3 pm. Dinner: 6 pm-midnight

FALCON HOTEL, Chapel Street   5777
Chef: Terry Maleary
   Solomugundy, 17
   Falcon green pepper steak, 36
Luncheon: 12.30-2 pm. Dinner: 6.15-9 pm

DA GIOVANNI RESTAURANT, Ely Street   297999
Chef: Giuseppe Alberti
   Escalopes Piemontese, 22
Luncheon: 12.30-2 pm. Dinner: 6.30-11.30 pm
(Closed Sun and Bank Holidays)

GROSVENOR HOUSE HOTEL, Warwick Road   69213
Chef: Paul Short
   Qiche Creole, 19
   Rognons d'agneau marchand de vins, 38
   Cauliflower royale, 40
   Cabbage creams, 42
   Luncheon: 12-1.45 pm. Dinner: 6-8.45 pm

**HATHAWAY TEA ROOMS
AND BAKERY**, High Street   292404
Chef: Marie Spiers
   Prawn and chive quiche, 19
   Amber tart, 43
   Merry cake, 51
   Apricot eggs, 51
Open: 9 am-5.30 pm (7 days)

HILTON INTERNATIONAL, Bridgefoot   67511
Chef: Brian Stamp
   Supreme of chicken with fresh asparagus, 27
Warwick Grill: 7-11 pm. Tavern Restaurant: 10 am-11.30 pm

MARIANNE RESTAURANT, Greenhill Street   293563
Chef: Thirza Denervaux
   Charlotte au chocolat, 50
Luncheon: 12.30-2 pm. Dinner: 7-11.30 pm

MARLOWE'S RESTAURANT, High Street   4999
Chef: Mr Anthony
  Terrine de poulet Lauretta Okagbue, 26
  Duck Aubriche, 28
Luncheon: 12-2.30 pm. Dinner 6-11.30 pm
Sun and Bank Holidays: Luncheon 12-2.30 pm
Dinner: 7-10.30 pm

ROSE AND CROWN, Sheep Street   297884
Chef: Gary Moss
  Medaillons de porc Selina, 23
  Open 8 am-midnight

ROYAL SHAKESPEARE THEATRE, Waterside   293226
BOX TREE RESTAURANT
Chef: Tony Carbonari
  Fillet of pork San Anton, 31
Luncheon: 12.30-2 pm (matinées and Sun).
Dinner: 6 pm-after performance (not Sun)

SHAKESPEARE HOTEL, Chapel Street   294771
Chef: Patrick Watson
  Baked avocado fruits de mer, 14
  Sanganaki à la Perea, 20
  Aliguillettes of chicken Indienne, 27
  Lemon cheese torten, 50
Luncheon: 12.30-2.15 pm.
Dinner: 6.15-9.45 pm (Sun, 7-9.30 pm)

SWAN'S NEST HOTEL, Bridgefoot   66761
BERWICK RESTAURANT
Chef: R. Wyatt
  Stilton and port pâté, 10
  Evesham asparagus, 14
  Celery, apple and tomato soup, 16
  Sole Old England, 20
  Fillets Bewick, 32
  Stratford syllabub, 43
Luncheon: 12.30-2 pm (7 days). Dinner 6.15-9.30 pm
(Sun, 6.30-9.30 pm)

WELCOMBE HOTEL, Warwick Road   295252
Chef: Michel Vallade
  Fircassée de sole aux moules à la crème de saffran, 21
  Fillet de boeuf à la ficelle, 37
Luncheon: 12.30-2.15 pm
Dinner: 7-9.15 pm (from 6 pm, not à la carte)

WHITE SWAN HOTEL, Rother Street   297022
REGENCY RESTAURANT
Chef: Stephen Gilkes
  Tournedos Olde England, 33
  Pineapple Regence, 46
Luncheon: 12-2 pm. Dinner: 6.15-8.30 pm

THE PLAYS OF WILLIAM SHAKESPEARE

William Shakespeare is thought to have written all his plays between 1590 and 1613. They are:

Henry VI (Parts I, II & III)	Twelfth Night; or What You Will
Richard III	Hamlet, Prince of Denmark
The Comedy of Errors	The Merry Wives of Windsor
Titus Andronicus	Troilus and Cressida
The Taming of the Shrew	All's Well That Ends Well
Love's Labour's Lost	Measure for Measure
The Two Gentlemen of Verona	Othello, The Moor of Venice
Romeo and Juliet	King Lear
Richard II	Macbeth
A Midsummer-Night's Dream	Antony and Cleopatra
King John	Coriolanus
The Merchant of Venice	Timon of Athens
Henry IV (Parts I & II)	Pericles
Much Ado About Nothing	Cymbeline
Henry V	The Winter's Tale
Julius Caesar	The Tempest
As You Like It	Henry VIII

"Good-night, good-night! parting is such sweet sorrow
That I shall say good-night till it be morrow."
ROMEO AND JULIET II.ii.184.

... we shall be up with the lark and going on more culinary rambles. Look out for other books in this series on your travels.

Available now:
The Bath Cookbook
Coming shortly:
The Cambridge Cookbook
The Oxford Cookbook

In preparation:
The Cotswolds Cookbook
The Kensington Cookbook
The York Cookbook
The Edinburgh Cookbook